DRIVE ON

DRIVE ON

A Chapbook

Richard P. Gabriel

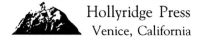 Hollyridge Press
Venice, California

Hollyridge Press
P.O. Box 2872
Venice, California 90294
www.hollyridgepress.com

Cover and Book Design by Rio Smyth
Author photo by Jo Lawless
Manufactured in the United States of America by Lightning Source

ISBN-13: 978-0-9752573-8-8
ISBN-10: 0-9752573-8-2

Grateful acknowledgment is made to the editor of the
publication in which the following poem first appeared:

Puerto Del Sol: "The Source of It All"

12 11 10 09 08 07 06 05   10 9 8 7 6 5 4 3 2 1

Contents

Drive On

TIME LEAVES

Wind-pearled leaves upturned on birches,
and leaves' papered veins' faint scrolls carry
dropped lines in mid-kiss, lips from old films,
lies spurting in fine print.

From across the weed-spattered field erupting life
in mites and speck flies, grasshoppers and light-clear moths, I stare
at those leaves, and even these binoculars, perfect and fine,
fail. And still between us, the fragments I need—life flares—
rise in the heat-perfume. Feet and fingers stop, lips
stop their glassy brush.

Dust and stalk-dry fragrance lull this lizard to a stillness
ready to break for shade. How far the trees stand
bending to a wind overhead.

THE SOURCE OF IT ALL

Even the day after death, air drains
to the floor as if the circle of wind
makes a difference; we sit
puzzled by the cold at our feet
in a room half-filled with the urge
to move, just any part of us
in any direction but the round
envelope of the air in the room. This time
I hung behind and watched grave workers pull away
the green carpets and lower by clever parts
the coffin into its box and lower half-lids
with fat ropes over the dark roses we left.
The pieces formed an imperfect seal they
covered with thin and dusty soil
which billowed like the flock of birds
that picked just then to head south. Two men
with shovels and a wind building to early snow. Make
that three. I'll tell you what it is:
The cold wind come down from Montreal cools
the winter glass, and air warmed by our grief
rises to meet the glass where it chills and falls
along the glass face, gaining speed as it gains cold,
draining to the floor, heavy as a lump of clay
mixed in dusty soil. Warm air is forced up
to the glass to circle, circle, to circle.
Have you ever smelled cold glass, winter
just beyond, smelled what it does to warm air?
Smell the cold glass, tell me what you smell.

FAITH SEED

Snow falls and where it ends, he thinks, all will.
Streets stop, dark gorges on the city, even
streetlight penetrates shallow the dark
where he leans shoulder to brick, knee bent and foot tucked,
hands pocketed and tight, everything he has
neatly put away against the cold—everything evaporated
to a bulb of streetlight whose shape is seen by tattered flakes,
every sound in the night swallowed and the song in his head faded.
Waiting at their meeting place for the woman who left him
just outside a small ring of faith that dimly lights his face,
he knows light can't be seen—it's as dark as what's lost—
unless you stand where it's aimed. He knows
this not by faith but by time
spent standing in the shade.

Or unless you stand where it scatters, where light
gone wrong in a bad-luck bounce lands by chance.
He knows this not from faith but from times spent sitting in night
dark rooms warmly lit by a streetlight's mild distraction,
lit by what the orange bright arc cares nothing of,
or little of.

(…somewhere else, in the metal-stained light of a streetlight's arc
a rained-on curb bursts orange and bare, but
in the room beyond, behind the thin curtain gauze,
after the mist sprinkles chance, the sprung-free light hangs
like a hushed song, like the last of her *shhh* as she closes
the door between them…)

He believes in faith, all but its size; he's seen
it angled, not head-on, caught only its side
as it passed nearby—as it passed while he stood in the shade.
Faith's flight is wide, and when it passes, the shade
lightens.

Outside the streetlight, a sound starts—
of steps and shifting shoes on the whitening curb,
light sounds coming near in the dark.
His hands pull free from what pocket warmth there was,
his boot slips down the brick and his knee unfolds.

He hears shoes stopping in the midst of the streetlight's orange arc;
he leans his shoulder forward and pushes up from the wall.
Toward the back of his mind he hears the sounds
of a serenade and steps into the rim of his streetlight,
he hears the *shhh* swell to faith.

THE LAST TO KNOW ALWAYS VANISHES

—For my family, just the two of them

I. Which You Is It?
Late November, the sky
held close, snow
drunk-walking down.
The gray thin maples at grass's verge
stood steady. Mother and Father butchered
a pig in the lowering sky light.

No sound
but the slice of knife through meat
like birth sliding out
and the murmuring words
of butchers at work.

II. Mother: House of Hard Hearing
Your house refused to be painted,
fell down instead—its fell-down beams holding
up against the bleach of deep noticing
reserved for children and bees. Did you think
I didn't see its nails rust and thin
till they snapped? Its foundation—
not dug, but sandy soil piled
against mortared rocks broken square—
is filled by debris
heaped on broken floors and half-hearted walls:
lamps I never saw lit, books you closed
as soon as I opened them, bits of plates
and cups you used for whispered meals
long after I fell to bed.
In that new-made dump I added my own
throw-aways: soup cans and letters,
apple cores and pictures of us. You said

to make a strong foundation wall
place an iron meteorite
in poured concrete and connect
an iron rod from its center to the surface
—hammer, and the blow
would ring hard, bursting
by vibration small caves of trapped air,
the voice of resonating metal
settling unstill forms. But that's all
you said. The back
of my hand is a wild place to see
the future and each hair
that turns white there is a year
the bedstead and springs creak
from hard rust and warm winds
not my jump for joy.

III. The Knife
A 9-inch slaughter knife,
thick blade, fresh sharp edge,
prepared to painlessly open
the flesh deep to the bone
at the back of a neck.

What kind of steel was it, which knife-smith
designed the blade,
forged it to follow the exact line
that separates a pig from its life?
What kind of thing could
so quickly move
between life and death?

IV. Father: Butterflies Gather and Rejoice
The beams were hand-hewn
but you never said by whose—the wood

well past brown and into gray
and generations of cows had so smoothed
the slats that held their necks in place
they were riverstones in a bowl of water.
By the time I thought to ask
so were you and your memories had shattered
like the south-facing boards you never painted.
After the hay was lined in rows
you backed the hay-rake under the barn
on the ground level side
and there it still sits after 30 years rusting
by the pool of urine-soaked water which gathers
every day after I wash down the cow stalls.
Your fingers grow curved like old paper or weed stalks.
But none of this explains the massed butterfly swarm
by the ditch that drains the pool beneath the barn
and sends the water—piss and all—to the seasonal stream
that draws what's left to the dispersing sea.
Your hands once smooth have hardened to boards
that move in tight-bound circles by your knees;
I know them only by their rasp touch on my cheek.
Your voice has washed into itself and dried to a pair of folded wings.
In the field, one by one, the butterflies drop
to a bare spot where they watch the sky fold to firey ash
and the barn drop its time-worn beams
on your last day's work and the waste left behind.

V. My Yearly Walk

I've long since left this valley behind,
but every year I return, stop by the river,
and up from bitter river smells
past sugar-filled trees I climb small rolled lawns
by upturned stones bearing names,
by gaps in straight headstone rows
where dead will some day lie. I seek
the piece of land they bought

among the boring long, same rows,
the place where they will be one day:
Through ten or twenty years of quiet,
gap-or-grave is their only message to me.
It takes a minute to find the gap.

Sometimes I want to find the gap, and sometimes
I want to find graves.
When I find the gap I stand in it
and look down toward the river
that flows with indecision both ways.
I pretend I still live in this valley.
I think: You're still alive
somewhere.

VI. The Meteorite Always Rings Twice
After you left I cleared the cellar,
heaped its contents in a hole I dug
by the stream. With the tips
of my fingers I checked the concrete walls
he poured for rods. Later,
while the sky dispersed to blurring shards,
I finger-combed my hair and thought
of what you said. I think

a hangman worked here once
and from that sun-cured joist
after the stool was kicked free
you held your breath instead.

Laments

LAMENT ONE DAY EARLY

Soon the way back
will dim away and there will be a limit.
                    The storyteller
                    is losing

her mind or is her
forgetting getting

                    better?
                    She practices

starving and not moving,
her answers are

                    no answers,
                    and I fear it.

There is one last loon
hiding in the scrub

                    waiting to
                    hoo hoo

once the blend of light and dark
is right enough. Mark the end
                    mark the end
                    (the loon cries)
                    mark the end.

LAMENT ONE DAY LATE

Imagine darkness falling
        head over heels for one
more has been added
        like drops of water and salt
to sea waves or a loon to a pond
        filling with loons.

Then it's time to wonder
        not knowing
what comes next
        what the cost will be
to open the door no matter
        how broken it is.

We'll scan the lines written
        not labored over
to find the ones that can never be forgotten
        then lose our way once more.

LAMENT OF ENCIRCLEMENT
AND APPROACH

we approach it like—
watching out for—

circling 10' outside
range uncertain

we sniff
the air is laden

one mystery—
—footprints buried

grass staining grass
only one good news

a robin poses and pines
on the branch nearby, her
nest filled with chicks whose mouths
open their nest is on a sill
where someone looked out

once
in an older time
when nests were large

LAMENT AFTER GOING IN

We've parked and take turns
holding her urn in the car.
We face the mountain
whose peak is classic—a rock cone
visible all the way
from this lakeside to heaven.
To the west a veil of powder-light clouds
leaks orange color as
through a gaping door that leads
to a world of glittering uncommonality.
The urn has turned gold in the light
and in our hope

that the way we've admitted
to sentimentalism will be taken
as a blessing when she needs
it most, maybe wants it least,
but at last it's just our way
to say goodnight to her
on the first of her last 2 or 3 nights
at home before we send her
closer to where she'll want to be
one day when she finds herself
not here.

LAMENT REPRESENTING ONGOING WORK

At the edge of a field filled
with round balls of lavender clover
a crew dismantles an oak,
starting at the top with the long branches
that trace the bottom of wind. After each branch
falls more trunk is taken down. The men
stop every 30 minutes to sit under the diminishing shade
and sip from jars of lemonade filled from one
of 5 big buckets, and when the shade is gone
they move their drinks and tools to the rim
of shade around the field. They climb like arboreals
or use ladders on the flat beds of a pair of trucks
to reach the limbs that go next. Later
the field fills with limbs and leaves
losing their lives while the wind finds
the way less obstructed and the lemonade
buckets grow more empty, less able to comfort
the sweating work of the men.

LAMENT UPON FORGETTING

Cleaning up is everyone's last duty,
and now memories begin their work
of forgetting—first details then the outline,
everything. Soaking in is a good
metaphor, for what soaks stains
as it marks and memorizes. Maybe
the carpet she stained for years can be cut apart
to keep what's right, and the forgettable burned,
but the edges might fray and unravel. Everything
unravels. The world remembers, the world changes.

Yesterday we drove past a pretty place
and forgot something sweet.

LAMENT OF CLOSING

Even the air, so soft, can jolt—
what once was wished for
is mourned—clouds, once
so soft, fill the air with rain,
with lightning, with pounding
and thunder—and the ground, once
so firm, has become liquid and settles
then flows down to the sea
like a procession. Everything left behind
is closed up, locked, and crippled to keep
the remaining change at bay, to limit
the expansion of the unknown.

Let's bottom out
the meanings of events
in the shards of memories and emotions
rampant when it was raining—
because some day it will stop,
the sun will be revealed,
and the way home will be the way
we become.

LAMENT ON WORK

There is working hard in death—
by the one who dies by
labored breathing and heavy movements,

or the beating heart pushing hard;
by the ones who clean up by
brushing hot caustic liquids through carpet plush,

or scraping from linoleum the last of it away;
by the ones who prepare by
digging holes, carving granite, marking unimportantly

on paper; by the ones who live by getting
by, and by doing so, pass close by
places of singularity in a frame unlike

our normal minds, wrapped in rigor;
by doing this we earn our lives; by
doing this...

LAMENT ON CIRCLING

we opened the garage and sat there
we found white lawn chairs and sat on them just inside the garage door
outside it seemed like many things were alive
maybe all of them

the house sealed up filled us with dread flowing somehow into us
the air became filled with grasshoppers and mites and birds flew by
carrying grubs and worms
we could hear a storm far away growing near
its flashing lights made an unsteady strobe
later that night we lay in bed without blinking while it rained
someone important was not listening

someone important was not watching
we opened the door
all our senses were on hold
we held on for dear life

the darkness would not move
the darkness would not move out
the darkness would not move out of the way

                    out
                        of the way

we saw a pattern that would not repeat
we circled the house until the moon rose and kept it up
until the loons flew by

have you ever driven a car over powdery dry dirt and it feels like floating?
think of that feeling and call it the looming compass
there is little else to go on

LAMENT ON THE REALITIES PICKING UP

She's vanished and her secrets
remain buried but stems and stalks poke out,
buds about to bloom, and
she's won't say how to nurture them
and trim them.
Again, I'm left with no facts,
no truth, only music.

She said the pile was this
high but I see only half of it,
and that half is thinned out
as if rain had washed part away.

She isn't what she used to be.
Her daddy told her
people would use her.
She and his warning squashed them. She was strong
till the end, but what did it gain her,
to be that strong
yet yield so little?

LAMENT ON DESIRE AND SATISFACTION

Clams: A food she once loved—
she savored them when she was young
then forsook them for 20 years, though the stands
stood by the road she drove every week.

I bought some her some before I left.
Cooking them is easy, done by novices
in the crudest way possible
almost. Clams were special to her.

Such things now just are,
like the plain facts written here, just information.
She sat there eating clams and smacking her lips;
my imagination filled her head
with desire and satisfaction.

LAMENT FOR GOODBYES

Here is what we see tonight
as the cool settles down
to become the halting night and stars do nothing
but hang: Night on earth is singing
with a voice that tenses
and relinquishes. In this sand
the trace remains of recent passing
and the warmth from their feet hangs on.

LAMENT ON THE BEAUTY OF PASSING

From my window I hear footsteps
approaching the fountain and its water
falling on stone and splitting in shards,

forming drops under the sun,
evaporating away like the throngs

of birds who leave the swarm and spin
away into the hidden caves of tree canopy.

Their eyes follow mine as I watch the water
flow away from sight and regard
the woman walking past whose walk

has straightened and steadied
as she casts off her other self
and becomes at last real.

LAMENT ON STORIES

I never saw her again
for the end was up in the trees

waiting when I left. She breathed shallowly
rather than confess. I looked for a kiss

and the gate was swung closed
even though its chain had been removed

forever. Did she wait for my call
to confess instead? I called.

How small was she? Light,
they said, was kept off

her face. On my birthday
birds will land and snails

will bellow as the sun rises;
a hoard awaits

in the pit of dreams
devoid of stories.

LAMENT OVER DREAMS

She had every big dream
and saw the lives of many launched.
The grass in front of her window
bowed in the rain and withered
in the sun. Insects
popped up, flew past blinding her sight
to what might have been visible
had the dreams been less thick.

LAMENT ON CONFRONTING
THE LANGUAGE OF STONE

I've been searching for right words,
not many and neither clever
nor hard—length is important,
how they fall in lines and how they read
when carved: The way the light falls on the lines
makes all the difference, what's in shade can reveal
what's in direct sun; what sense do they take on
when rain has soaked into them or snow hangs
from their little loops.

LAMENT UPON ART'S INABILITY TO MUTE

The celebration unfolds,
emotions bursting like a spate of butterflies

alarmed suddenly and together

from a patch of buddelia
planted for decoration
by an artificial pond.

Their colors individually assertive
combine in their flush and our inattention
to churn a gold butter that fans
before the staged pond water
and the leaking liner of the pond

in a way that links the celebration,
the laughter, the downward stares,
and the dead with the grasp of comprehension
through the mechanism called
artistic falsehood.

LAMENT AFTER LORCA

The robin who laid her eggs
while you were still here
has forgotten you, the fear
you felt over thunderstorms
from the time lightning shot
past your eyes has forgotten
you, the carpets you swept
when you could not walk
have forgotten you, the water
bubbling from the well
we dug when all else failed
doesn't know you, the heat
and wet from the South wind
will not look into your eyes,
the cool wet fog that surrounds even now
your house has no idea of you
any more—all of them are condensed
in me who heard your last laments
and prayers for everything to cease,
and like all the dead of the earth
you are just a story I and one
or two others will tell for a short
time, less than the time it took
you to die.

LAMENT ON THE END OF LAMENTS

Sunset stimulates indecision
as we move away from the celebration
and through alleys bounded by houses
decaying and lowering themselves
nail by nail into the cobblestones—
she's been buried and careful words
were spoken over her today.

Sunset bars our way by holding
out hope that within the end
something beautiful awaits
after the darkness is shushed away
and the rainclouds break for the coast.

Sunset hooks us by the lapels
and we're reduced to pacing
and by pacing counting and
by counting replacing
our memories with stories
whose passion imprisons the
hopeful gathered indecisively.

Say It Anyway

ABSTRACT IN MEMORIAM

Someone died secretly
and was quickly laid to rest;

he spoke quietly making real sense
out of nonsense but liked to drive way
too fast. No one released the details

of his death though the cremation
is known and so the disposal, but

the force of his ideas or should I say
the soft pockets of still clarity

are drifting like the smoke of an ornamental
fire made of cedar sticks and aromatics

and soon the sky will change shades
just this little.

MOTHER REMEMBERS THE DAY
THE PRINCIPAL SCORNED HER

She sleeps in a cocoon
in a cold room though the night outside
is warm on the verge of hot. The insulation
works too well, and the windows represent the wrong
tradeoff between strength and light. Afternoon
forces her to bed. She grows more tired each day from hard sleep.
She grows thin for who can eat while sleeping?

> The flight, the drive, the walk,
> breaking in,
> cleaning up,
> lighting up,
> warming up,
> locking up,
> the walk, the drive, the flight.

Today is cool on the verge
of warm. Butterflies lock their wings
into neutral and form their lenses
in the pines. Loons float in shadows
peeking at the sun, motionless on the verge
of flight. The wind and sun in the pines
and I watch over these signs and wait,
wait, wait,
wait,

wait,

wait.

DADDY

My hope is to see him again,
not alive but something like
it, when he felt confident
and not alone. when he was strong
and not on his knees wondering
who to pray to, when he didn't have to stare
into the woods to swallow
his pride, when he didn't need
to hide what he loved, when he could understand
what it meant to live and didn't need
to be told.

SONG/(DREAM AND BLESSING)

One day my daughter will die
with long memories I can never know
filled with love for strangers
in a town I'll never be to
in a bed, I hope, made up lovingly
by people I can't imagine who hold her
tenderly, who find her a blessing,
after her head unfolds thoughts
I could never have, after a life
defining people who today
can only stumble and mutter. With all the words
I can find and lines I can write in wild profusion,
in all my clever thinking and imagining,
with all the books I've written and postures, the incredible
singing I've heard and playing I've done and places
I've been and people I've loved and hated,
all the muscle work for nothing much
I've tried to picture the tint of purple
on the iris outside the window where she'll
breathe in her last and with that last breath
say a word that some will write down
and others never forget, but I can't:
that day is too removed, my simplicity
too limiting, my reach no wider
than her wrist the day I first brought
her home and all she could dream of
was me.

LONG BY THE SEA

I walk at the end
of a long day ending
by a strongly rolling sea
my breath has been eased
and my lungs are filling full
with the crisp and salted air

after a hard dusk
    of a storm sky breaking
    of a storm sky spanning
    of the birds huddling among the roots
    of straining trees
the steep last rising
face of the storm
is slowly then forgotten

what hurt the storm brings
is slowly then forgotten
and I am not
remembering the long climbs
no more detained
I am the runner who once ran past

the path here twisting through many woods
did the dawn once open up
long ago
is the sea air clearing

once frozen lips
are melting
eyes fading along the sea
right now

my hand feels the long grip of yours
pass away
I hear the boom and fall of the nearby sea
I feel the need pass by me
as the storm moves over a distant hill

find the dusk and open up
say it anyway
leave me here
walking at the end of a long day
remembering what I've forgotten
long ago
along the sea

Printed in the United States
35240LVS00008B/34-51